Facilitator's Guide

HOW THE
Special Needs
Brain Learns

SECOND EDITION

David A. Sousa

CORWIN PRESS
A SAGE Publications Company
Thousand Oaks, CA 91320

For information:

Corwin Press
A Sage Publications Company
2455 Teller Road
Thousand Oaks, California 91320
www.corwinpress.com

Sage Publications Ltd.
1 Oliver's Yard
55 City Road
London EC1Y 1SP
United Kingdom

Sage Publications India Pvt. Ltd.
B-42, Panchsheel Enclave
Post Box 4109
New Delhi 110 017 India

Printed in the United States of America on acid-free paper

ISBN 978-1-4129-5287-3

07 08 09 10 9 8 7 6 5 4 3 2 1

Acquisitions Editor:	Robert D. Clouse
Editorial Assistant:	Jessica Wochna
Production Editor:	Sanford Robinson
Typesetter:	C&M Digitals (P) Ltd.
Cover Designer:	Scott Van Atta

Contents

About the Author

**David A. Sousa,** EdD, is an international educational consultant. He has made presentations at national conventions of educational organizations and has conducted workshops on brain research and science education in hundreds of school districts and at several colleges and universities across the United States, Canada, Europe, and Asia.

Dr. Sousa has a bachelor of science degree in chemistry from Massachusetts State College at Bridgewater, a master of arts in teaching degree in science from Harvard University, and a doctorate from Rutgers University. His teaching experience covers all levels. He has taught high school science, served as a K–12 director of science, and was Supervisor of Instruction for the West Orange, New Jersey, schools. He then became superintendent of the New Providence, New Jersey, public schools. He has been an adjunct professor of education at Seton Hall University and a visiting lecturer at Rutgers University. He was president of the National Staff Development Council in 1992.

Dr. Sousa has edited science books and published numerous books and articles in leading educational journals on staff development, science education, and brain research. He has received awards from professional associations and school districts for his commitment and contributions to research, staff development, and science education. He received the Distinguished Alumni Award and an honorary doctorate in education from Bridgewater (Mass.) State College.

He has appeared on the NBC *Today* show and on National Public Radio to discuss his work with schools using brain research. He makes his home in south Florida.

Introduction

This facilitator's guide is a companion for *How the Special Needs Brain Learns, Second Edition*, by David A. Sousa. It is designed to accompany the study of the book and provide assistance to group facilitators, such as school leaders, professional development coordinators, peer coaches, team leaders, mentors, and professors. Along with a summary of each chapter in the book, David A. Sousa has provided supplemental information, chapter discussion questions, activities, and journal-writing prompts. For facilitators who conduct workshops, a sample workshop evaluation form is also included.

When using the guide during independent study, focus on the summaries and discussion questions.

For small study groups, the facilitator should guide the group through the chapter work.

For small or large group workshops, the facilitator should create an agenda by selecting activities and discussion starters from the chapter reviews that meet the group's goals and guide the group through the learning process.

Corwin Press also offers a free 16-page resource titled *Tips for Facilitators* which includes practical strategies and tips for guiding a successful meeting. The information in this resource describes different professional development opportunities, the principles of effective professional development, some characteristics of an effective facilitator, the responsibilities of the facilitator, and useful ideas for powerful staff development. *Tips for Facilitators* is available for free download at the Corwin Press website (www.corwin press.com, under "Extras").

Chapter-by-Chapter Study Guide
How the Special Needs Brain Learns, Second Edition

By David A. Sousa

Summary

- Educators are searching for new strategies and techniques to meet the needs of an ethnically, culturally, and socially diverse student population. Some tried-and-true strategies are not as successful as they were in the past, and more students seem to be having difficulty acquiring just the basic skills of reading, writing, and computation.
- For the purposes of this book, the term "special needs" refers to students who are (1) diagnosed and classified as having specific learning problems, including speech, reading, writing, mathematics, and emotional and behavioral disorders; (2) enrolled in supplemental instruction programs for basic skills, such as those receiving federal funding under Title 1 of the Elementary and Secondary Education Act; and (3) not classified for special education nor assigned to Title I programs, but still struggling with problems affecting their learning.
- This book discusses brain research that relates to teaching and learning, especially as it applies to students with learning difficulties. Some of these research findings are challenging long-held beliefs about the cause, progress, and treatment of specific

learning disorders. Educators in both general and special education should be aware of this research so that they can decide what implications the findings have for their practice.

- Some students designated as "learning disabled" may be merely "schooling disabled." Sometimes, these students are struggling to learn in an environment that is designed inadvertently to frustrate their efforts. Just changing our instructional approach may be enough to move these students to the ranks of successful learners.
- Several chapters contain lists of symptoms that are used to help identify specific disorders. The symptoms are included only for informational purposes and they should not be used as a basis for diagnosis. Any individual who exhibits persistent learning problems should be referred to qualified clinical personnel for assessment.

Discussion Questions

1. How does this book define students with special needs?

2. In what ways can general and special education teachers collaborate to help students with special needs?

3. What does the author mean by stating that some students who are labeled "learning disabled" may just be "schooling disabled"?

Chapter 1: The Brain and Learning

Summary

- Important exterior regions of the brain include the frontal, temporal, occipital, and parietal lobes; the motor cortex; and the somatosensory cortex.
- Other structures include the brainstem, limbic system, cerebrum, cerebellum, and brain cells. The structures in the limbic (emotional) area mature by the early teens. But those in the frontal lobe responsible for controlling emotions mature much later, explaining why adolescents often resort to high-risk behavior.
- Scientists have discovered clusters of neurons firing just before a person carries out a planned movement. These neurons also fired when a person saw someone else perform the movement. Thus, similar brain areas process both the production and perception of movement. Called mirror neurons, they may help an individual to decode the intentions and predict the behavior of others. Neuroscientists believe that mirror neurons may explain

a lot about mental behaviors, such as autism, that have remained a mystery.

- Learning occurs when the synapses make physical and chemical changes so that the influence of one neuron on another also changes. When a set of neurons "learns" to fire together, then repeated firings make successive firings easier. Eventually, the firing becomes automatic and a memory is formed.

- Learning involves the brain, the nervous system, and the environment, and the process by which their interplay acquires information and skills. Sometimes, we need information for just a short period of time, and then the information decays after just a few seconds. Thus, learning does not always involve or require long-term retention. Retention requires that the learner give conscious attention and build conceptual frameworks that have sense and meaning for consolidation into long-term memory.

- Because students with learning disabilities can have difficulty focusing for very long, teachers of these students must emphasize why they need to learn certain material. Meaning (or relevancy) becomes the key to focus, learning, and retention. Retention is an inexact process influenced by many factors including the degree of student focus, the length and type of rehearsal that occurred, the critical attributes that may have been identified, the student's learning style, the impact of any learning disabilities, and the inescapable influence of prior learning.

- Rote rehearsal is used when learners need to remember and store information or a skill in a specific form or sequence. We employ rote rehearsal to remember a poem, the lyrics and melody of a song, multiplication tables, telephone numbers, and steps in a procedure. Elaborative rehearsal is used when it is unnecessary to store information exactly as learned, and when it is important to associate new learnings with prior learnings to detect relationships. Here, learners review the information several times to make connections to previous learnings and assign meaning. Students use rote rehearsal to memorize a poem but elaborative rehearsal to interpret its message.

- Scanning studies show that a person uses the frontal lobe, motor cortex, and cerebellum while learning a new physical skill. Learning a motor skill involves following a set of procedures and can be eventually carried out largely without conscious attention. Children with low motor ability will have difficulty learning motor skills. But it is a mistake to assume that low motor ability also means low perceptual or intellectual ability.

- The brain of today's student has developed in an environment filled with interactive as well as passive technology. It has become acclimated to novelty. Educators need to consider ways in which they can include novelty as part of the learning approaches that are used in school, especially when dealing with students who have special learning needs.

Discussion Questions

1. What are the four major lobes of the brain and the primary function of each?

2. How do neurons transmit impulses to other neurons?

3. What are mirror neurons and why are they significant?

4. How are learning and retention different?

5. Describe rote and elaborative rehearsals. Give some examples of when you would use each type of rehearsal.

6. What is meant by novelty? How is leisure time used by children today different from when you were a child? What impact do these differences have on the developing brain?

Activity

● *Review of Brain Areas and Functions* (p. 6)

Time: 15 minutes

Materials: *How the Special Needs Brain Learns*, Second Edition

Give the participants about 10 minutes to study the brain diagram on page 6 of the book. Ask them to get up and walk across the room, find a partner, and alternate sharing their understanding of each one of the brain structures in the diagram and their functions. Repeat this process for the diagram on page 9.

Chapter 2: When Learning Difficulties Arise

Summary

- Possible causes of learning disabilities include genetic links; tobacco, alcohol, and other drug use; problems during pregnancy or delivery; and toxins and stress in the child's environment.
- There are many more boys than girls diagnosed with learning difficulties, dyslexia, and autism. Possible explanations are (1) Male fetuses are more likely than female fetuses to invoke a foreign-body response by the mother's immune system, setting up a hostile womb environment that leads to fetal brain damage.

(2) If a substance, such as testosterone, slows the formation of the brain's cortex, then male fetuses would be more susceptible than female fetuses.

(3) Certain brain deficits affecting learning result from genetic mutations on the X chromosome. Females have two X chromosomes, so the healthy chromosome can prevent the unwanted effects of the mutated one. Males possess only one X chromosome, and thus suffer the full consequences of any mutations on that chromosome.

- Many children who are gifted in some ways and deficient in others go undetected and unserved by their schools. They tend to fall through the cracks because the system is not designed to deal with such widely different conditions occurring in the same student. About two to five percent of all students are likely to be gifted and also have learning disabilities. Researchers continue to search for measurement activities that will accurately identify children with both talents and learning disabilities.

- *Responsiveness to Intervention* (RTI) identifies students with learning difficulties by assessing whether their responses to the strategies, curriculum, and interventions they encounter lead to increased learning and appropriate progress. Proponents believe this problem-solving approach reduces student referrals and the overidentification of minority students, focuses on student outcomes with increased accountability, and promotes shared responsibility and collaboration. Critics argue that RTI focuses too much on reading disability, neglects the evaluation of psychological processes, cannot discriminate between students with learning disabilities and those whose learning problems are due to other factors, and fails to cover the whole range of age levels from preschool to high school.

- Students who have learning disabilities are often overwhelmed, disorganized, and frustrated in new learning situations. They often have difficulty following directions, have trouble with the visual or auditory perception of information, and have problems performing school tasks such as writing compositions, taking notes, doing written homework, or taking paper-and-pencil tests.

- Too often, students with learning problems believe that they cannot learn, that school tasks are just too difficult and not worth the effort, or that any success they do have is due to luck. They do not believe that there is a connection between the effort they make and the likelihood of academic success.

- Teachers should help students with learning disabilities decide which learning strategies to use in a particular situation. Learning skills develop when students receive opportunities to discuss, reflect upon, and practice cognitive and metacognitive strategies with classroom materials and appropriate skills.

- School-based interventions designed to boost the self-esteem of students with learning disabilities can be very effective. Researchers found that interventions using counseling techniques as well as both skill development and self-enhancement raised self-esteem. Effective academic interventions emphasized students working with their classmates and receiving feedback from classmates on their progress.

Supplemental Information

Urban air contains high concentrations of chemicals from vehicle exhausts, power plants, and tobacco smoke. A recent study at Columbia University found that babies born to women who breathed polluted urban air had a greater number of chromosomal abnormalities than babies of mothers who breathed cleaner air. Newborns in the low-exposure group had 4.7 abnormalities per 1,000 cells, while the highest-exposure group had 7.2 abnormalities per 1,000 cells. These abnormalities put the newborn at higher risk of cancer.

Other reasons why there are so many more boys than girls identified with learning disabilities center around how teachers interpret the different behaviors of boys and girls. Young boys who are just bored are much more likely than girls to be restless and resort to overt off-task behavior, which teachers may interpret as resulting from developmental problems with attention and controlling behavior. Meanwhile, young girls tend to deal with boredom quietly and in covert ways. Thus, more boys than girls get referred for evaluation not because they have a true learning disability but because the teacher's instructional style is not meeting their learning needs.

Adolescents who take recreational drugs can develop learning problems. Marijuana, for example, affects the parts of the developing brain that control behavior and cognitive functioning. Of particular concern is that marijuana use makes adolescents more vulnerable to heroin addiction later in life. The drug MDMA, also called ecstasy, can damage brain cells. Animal studies show that in doses taken by the typical adolescent, ecstasy killed neurons that make dopamine. This neurotransmitter is responsible for controlling movement as well as emotional and cognitive responses. Apparently, just a few doses can cause life-long damage to these neurons.

Students who are gifted and also have a learning disability are probably the most underidentified and underserved students in a school district. The lowest estimate is that these students represent about two percent of the school population. In a district of 5,000 students, that is 100 students. What are districts doing to identify and serve these students?

Discussion Questions

1. Describe some possible causes of learning disabilities.

2. What are some possible explanations for the much higher number of boys identified with learning disabilities than girls?

3. What methods are being used in my school or district to identify students who are gifted and who also have a learning disability?

4. How does the responsiveness-to-intervention approach differ from the earlier ability-achievement discrepancy criterion? What are the advantages and disadvantages of each approach?

5. What are examples of simple and complex learning strategies?

6. What are examples of cognitive and metacognitive learning strategies?

7. What does the research say about the effectiveness of learning strategies in working with students who have learning difficulties?

8. Explain the effectiveness of strategies designed to raise self-esteem.

Activities

● *Guidelines for Working With Students Who Have Special Needs* **(p. 37)**

Time: 20 minutes, with reading

Materials: *How the Special Needs Brain Learns,* Second Edition

Ask the participants to read "Guidelines for Working With Students Who Have Special Needs" on page 37. When completed, ask them to walk across the room and, working in pairs, review these eight guidelines with a partner. They should feel free to add any other guidelines they think would be appropriate. Provide an opportunity for the participants to share these added guidelines with the entire group.

● *Strategies for Involvement and Retention* **(pp. 38–39)**

Time: 25 minutes, with reading

Materials: Paper, pens, *How the Special Needs Brain Learns,* Second Edition

Ask the participants to read "Strategies for Involvement and Retention" on pages 38–39 before starting this activity, and then to select two strategies from the list that they think are particularly effective. (Perhaps they have used them or seen them used effectively.) Divide into groups of three and ask each group to select a reporter. (As an alternative to having the group select the reporter, you can suggest that the reporter is the person who meets some specific criteria in the group, for example, is the shortest or tallest, has the darkest hair, lives farthest from the workshop site, etc.)

The participants briefly explain in their small group why they chose their two strategies. Give the groups about 10 minutes for this discussion. The reporters then summarize their group's discussion for the entire group. Discuss reasons why some strategies were selected more often than others, and, if appropriate, why some strategies were not selected by any group.

Journal Writing: What two specific involvement or retention strategies will I use to help me deal successfully with students who have learning difficulties? Why do I think they will be effective?

● *Understanding the Strategies Integration Model (SIM) (pp. 32–33)*

Time: 30 minutes, with reading

Materials: Chart paper, markers, *How the Special Needs Brain Learns,* Second Edition

Ask the participants to suggest a few learning strategies that would be suited to the Strategies Integration Model (SIM). (See pages 32–33 in the text for examples of learning strategies.) Write their suggestions on chart paper. Select a strategy from the list that would be appropriate for all, or most, of the participants.

Divide the participants into six groups, and number the groups from one to six. Have each group select a recorder and presenter (or you can select them at random). Give each group chart paper and markers. Ask the group members to read silently the step in *Teaching Students to Use Learning Strategies* on pages 40–43 that corresponds to their group number (Group 1 reads Step 1, Group 2 reads Step 2, etc.). When they finish reading, they should discuss what specific activities they think are appropriate to carry the selected strategy through their step.

On the chart paper, the recorder writes the step number and name (as in the diagram on page 40) and an outline of the activities the group discussed. Starting with Group 1, the presenter displays the chart paper and explains to the whole group what that step is all about and how it would be used with the selected strategy. The other group presenters follow in numerical order.

Journal Writing: What learning strategy would I like to try with the Strategies Integration Model, and how would I do it?

● *Techniques for Building Self-Esteem* **(pp. 44–45)**

Time: 20 minutes

Materials: Paper, pens, *How the Special Needs Brain Learns,* Second Edition

Display the following scale on a sheet of chart paper or on an overhead projector:

1 (*Rarely*)——— 2 (*Sometimes*)——— 3 (*Regularly*)——— NA (*Does not apply*)

Ask the participants to read the list of techniques for building self-esteem on pages 44–45. They should use the scale to rate themselves on how often they use each technique in their classrooms or school. Give them about 10 minutes to complete this task. Then ask them to reflect on any items that received a score of 1. When done, ask the group if anyone wants to share an "Aha!" they may have had as a result of this activity.

Journal Writing: What *purposeful* steps will I take to help build self-esteem in my students?

Chapter 3: Attention Disorders

Summary

- Getting the brain's attention requires the coordination of three neural networks: alerting, orienting, and executive control. Alerting occurs in the brain stem and helps suppress background stimuli and inhibit ongoing activity. Orienting mobilizes neural resources to turn toward and process the expected input while inhibiting the transmission of all other input. Executive control links the limbic centers and directs the processes needed to decide how to respond. Problems can arise anywhere within these systems, and the resulting loss of attention may be accompanied by hyperactivity and impulsivity.
- Attention-deficit hyperactivity disorder (ADHD) interferes with an individual's ability to focus (inattention), regulate activity level (hyperactivity), and inhibit behavior (impulsivity). It affects an estimated five percent of youths ages 9 to 17, and is

about three times more prevalent in boys than girls. ADHD usually becomes evident in preschool or early elementary years, frequently persisting into adolescence and adulthood. Most adults outgrow the hyperactivity part of ADHD.

- Diagnosing ADHD involves a physical examination, a variety of psychological tests, and the observable behaviors in the child's everyday settings. These behaviors are compared to a list of symptoms contained in the fourth edition of the *Diagnostic and Statistical Manual of Mental Disorders (DSM–IV)*. A diagnosis of ADHD requires that six or more of the symptoms for inattention or for hyperactivity-impulsivity be present for at least 6 months, appear before the child is 7 years old, and be evident across at least two of the child's environments (e.g., at home, in school, on the playground, etc.).

- The exact causes of ADHD remain unknown. However, scientific evidence indicates that this is a neurologically based medical problem resulting from differences in brain structure and function as well as the presence of certain genetic abnormalities.

- Some children diagnosed with ADHD simply have the symptoms that mimic the disorder but do not have the disorder. Factors that can produce ADHD-like symptoms include watching too much television, not learning the acceptable and unacceptable rules of behavior in school, developing allergic reactions to foods that result in hyperactive behavior, lack of sleep, or reacting to stress or intolerant schools.

- Treatment for ADHD continues to be essentially through medication. However, alternative approaches, such as computer programs and behavioral therapy, are showing promise.

Supplemental Information

Researchers continue to debate whether attention deficit disorder (ADD) is a separate disorder from ADHD or merely a variation of it. Some are suggesting that the next major revision of the *Diagnostic and Statistical Manual of Mental Disorder* reclassify ADD as a variation of ADHD and rename it ADND for attention-deficit nonhyperactivity disorder. Others state that ADD has enough unique symptoms and variations that it should stand alone as a separate, but related, disorder. Stay tuned.

The increase in ADHD to about 5 percent of the student population is not peculiar to the United States. For example, the American Psychiatric Association recently reported that the prevalence of ADHD symptoms in school-aged children is 17 percent in Germany, 7.5 percent in Australia, and 6.5 percent in Thailand.

Discussion Questions

1. What systems in the brain are required to achieve attention and what is the function of each?

2. Describe the three primary symptoms of ADHD.

3. How does ADD differ from ADHD?

4. What are some of the possible causes of ADHD?

5. Under what conditions could a child display ADHD-like symptoms but not have true ADHD?

6. In what ways could schools induce ADHD-like behavior in students?

Activities

● *Avoiding Instructional Strategies That Lead to School-Created ADHD-Like Behavior* (p. 57)

Time: 20 minutes

Materials: *How the Special Needs Brain Learns*, Second Edition

Have the participants individually complete the instrument on page 57 by circling their responses. Then ask them to connect the circles from top to bottom to get a visual profile. Organize the participants in pairs and have them discuss their results with their partners, using the explanations on page 58 as part of their discussions. When completed, ask for any comments that participants are willing to share with the entire group.

Journal Writing: What strategies will I use or avoid so that my school/classroom does not create ADHD-like behavior in my students?

● *Strategies for Working With Students With ADHD/ADD* (p. 59)

Time: 30 minutes

Materials: Chart paper, markers, *How the Special Needs Brain Learns*, Second Edition

Organize the participants into job-alike groups as much as possible: Elementary teachers of the same grade level (or two) form a group. Group secondary teachers by subject area, others by job role (principals and assistant principals together, special education teachers together, etc.). No group should have more than five people. Give each group chart paper and markers.

Each group's task is to take 15 minutes to review the strategies on page 59 for working with students with ADHD/ADD and decide which ones are most appropriate for the students they work with. They are also free to add strategies that are not on the list. A recorder writes these briefly on chart paper. When completed, each small group presents its work to the entire group. The report should stress why the selected strategies are most appropriate for their students.

A further extension of this activity would be to ask participants if there are any strategies that they have used with students who have ADHD/ADD that they have found to be particularly effective. Any that were not? Why?

Journal Writing: What are two strategies I already use that are helpful for students with ADHD/ADD? What are two new strategies I will try with these students?

➥ *Getting, Focusing, and Maintaining Attention* (pp. 60–61)

Time: 30 minutes

Materials: Paper, pens, *How the Special Needs Brain Learns,* Second Edition

The goal of this activity is to give each member of a group of three a set time to become well versed in one of the three components of attention. At the end of the allotted time, each person will teach the other two about that component so that all become familiar with the entire process.

Organize the participants into groups of three and ask each group to designate Person 1, Person 2, and Person 3. (If a group has a fourth member, that person should select a component and be prepared to give the group specific classroom examples of the strategies listed.) The participants should open their books to pages 60–61. For the next 10 minutes, Person 1 silently reads "Getting Student Attention," Person 2 reads "Focusing Student Attention," and Person 3 reads "Maintaining Student Attention." While reading their sections, they should write down specific examples of how they have used some of the strategies listed. Remind the groups periodically of their remaining time for quiet reading.

When time is up, Person 1 takes 5 minutes to teach the other two group members about getting student focus, citing specific examples. Then Person 2 does the next section, and so on, until all three have presented their component.

Journal Writing: What are some specific strategies I use (or will use) to get, focus, and maintain student attention in the classroom?

Chapter 4: Speech Disabilities

Summary

- Many researchers believe that the ability to learn language is prewired in the brain at birth. Thus, spoken-language acquisition is a relatively easy task, and may be the result of a genetic predisposition coupled with the baby brain's incredible ability to identify regular sound patterns from background noise.
- Phonemes are the basic sounds of a language. By the age of 10 to 12 months, the toddler's brain has begun to distinguish and remember phonemes of the native language and to ignore nonnative sounds.
- The next step is to detect words. Babies begin to distinguish word boundaries by the age of 8 months and acquire new vocabulary words at the rate of about ten a day. At the same time, memory and Wernicke's areas are becoming fully functional so the child can now attach meaning to words. During the following years, practice in speaking and adult correction help the child decode some of the mysteries of grammar's irregularities and a language system emerges.
- Letting a toddler watch television does not accomplish the goal of phoneme discrimination, because the child's brain needs live human interaction to attach meaning to words. Moreover, television talk is not the slow, expressive speech that parents use with their infants. Other evidence indicates that prolonged television watching can impair the growth of young brains. The visual system is not stimulated properly by television viewing in that there is no pupil dilation and the eyes stare at the screen and do not move from one point to the next—a skill critical for reading. The images change quickly, robbing the higher-thought areas of the brain of the chance to process them. A television tube's wavelengths of light are very limited compared to the full spectrum of light when viewing objects outdoors.
- The successful use of oral language requires the brain to produce sounds that follow the rules for phonology, morphology, syntax, semantics, prosody, and pragmatics. Problems can occur. Some may just be a matter of time, while others may be more persistent due to physiological difficulties, childhood trauma, genetic influences, or other factors not yet understood.
- Problems in learning spoken language include language delay, specific language impairment, expressive language disorder,

receptive language disorder, adolescent language disorder, and stuttering.

- Students with language difficulties should not be discouraged from learning a second language. It is important to note, however, that the difficulties these students will have in acquiring another language stem from deficits in their first language.

Supplemental Information

There are differences in the way male and female brains process language. Male brains tend to process language in the left hemisphere, while most female brains process language in both hemispheres. Another interesting gender difference is that the large bundle of neurons that connects the two hemispheres and allows them to communicate (called the *corpus callosum*) is proportionately larger and thicker in the female than in the male. Assuming function follows form, this difference implies that information travels between the two cerebral hemispheres more efficiently in females than in males. The combination of dual-hemisphere language processing and more efficient between-hemisphere communications may account for why young girls generally acquire spoken language easier and more quickly than young boys. For more information on these gender differences in language see *How the Brain Learns to Read* (David A. Sousa, Corwin Press, 2005).

Recent research on the causes of specific language impairment is homing in on how rapidly an infant processes auditory cues. It seems that infants as young as 8 months who have difficulty processing auditory cues are likely to demonstrate language delays by the age of 3. Whether these findings can be used for diagnosis or to suggest interventions will be the subject of further research.

Discussion Questions

1. Why do scientists say that acquiring spoken language is a "natural ability"?

2. What are the steps involved in learning spoken language?

3. How does watching television affect language acquisition and the development of other abilities in toddlers?

4. Describe the different types of language disorders found in children and adolescents.

5. Should students with language deficits be taught a second language? Why or why not? What problems might they encounter?

Activity

➤ *Developing Oral Language Skills* (pp. 79–80)

Time: 20 to 30 minutes

Materials: Chart paper, markers, *How the Special Needs Brain Learns*, Second Edition

Organize the participants into six discussion groups. Number the groups one through six. (Groups that are too large for meaningful discussion should be divided into smaller groups and assigned the same number.) Each group designates a recorder. The participants should open their books to pages 79–80. Give each group chart paper and markers.

For the next 10 minutes, each group discusses the skill set listed in *Developing Oral Language Skills* that corresponds to the group's number (that is, Group 1 discusses "1. Talk to the Child," Group 2 discusses "2. Read to the Child," etc.). The discussion should focus on how the listed skills actually enhance the acquisition of spoken language. Group members can add other skills that they believe are appropriate for their category. The recorder should write on the chart paper how the skills in the group's category **promote** language acquisition.

When completed, each recorder reports to the entire group, starting with Group 1 and following in numerical order. Ask the recorders whether their group added other skills to the list and to share them with the entire group.

Journal Writing: What are two things I learned from this discussion on developing oral language skills that will help me in my teaching (or parenting)?

Chapter 5: Reading Disabilities

Summary

- Unlike spoken language, reading is not a natural ability, so there are no areas of the brain that specialize in reading. To read, the brain must recruit regions that are specialized for other purposes. Thus, reading is probably the most difficult task the young brain undertakes.
- Before children learn to read, they acquire vocabulary by listening to others and by practicing the pronunciation and usage of

new words in conversation. Children with language impairments are at risk for problems when learning to read.

- Reading involves two basic operations: decoding and comprehension. To decode, the student needs to possess phonemic awareness, understand phonics, and have an adequate vocabulary (mental lexicon). To comprehend, the student must know what the words in that lexicon mean and be able to decode with reasonable fluency.

- Reading involves cooperation among three neural systems: the visual-processing system, the auditory-processing system, and the executive system.

- Difficulties in learning to read can stem from social and cultural causes as well as from physical causes.

- Physical causes can be linguistic or nonlinguistic. Linguistic causes include phonological deficits, differences between auditory and visual processing speeds, structural differences in the brain, working memory deficits, genetic defects, brain lesions, and word-blindness. Nonlinguistic causes include poor perception of sequential sounds, inability to discriminate certain sound frequencies or to detect sounds from background noise, and deficits in the cerebellum resulting in poor motor coordination.

- Brain-imaging studies have revealed differences in both the structure and function of brains with dyslexia compared to typical brains. These investigations may lead to more accurate diagnosis and treatment.

- Detecting reading problems is not an easy task. However, there may be early signs of such problems when children have spoken-language delays or difficulties, or when they fail to respond to reading interventions in Grades 1 and 2.

- Recent research studies have demonstrated that, with intensive work, it is possible to rewire the brains of children with dyslexia so that they more closely resemble typical brains when reading. Commercial computer programs are available for struggling readers, which incorporate some of this research.

- Reading Recovery, Success for All, and The READ 180 Program are among the reading programs that have resulted in significant improvement in reading skills.

Supplemental Information

This chapter is designed to show how difficult it is to acquire reading skills compared to learning spoken language and to outline the major problems some students will encounter when learning to read.

Research on how to help students with reading difficulties suggests that teaching reading should focus on the following main ideas: phonemic awareness, phonics, vocabulary, comprehension, and fluency. Instructional methods should include explicit and direct instruction, scaffolded strategies (substantial support in the early stages of reading), and numerous opportunities for targeted practice and high-quality feedback. There should be specific performance indicators at each grade level and timely interventions based on the needs of individual students.

Perhaps no other curriculum area has benefitted more from neuroscience research than understanding how the brain learns to read. Not only has this research clarified the neural mechanisms at work during reading, but it has also evaluated the effects of interventions designed to rewire the brain of struggling readers to resemble more the brain of a typical reader.

Discussion Questions

1. Discuss the meaning of the following statement: Learning spoken language is a natural ability; reading is not.

2. What is the alphabetic principle? What impact does it have on learning to read?

3. Describe the three neural systems involved in reading.

4. How can social and cultural factors cause reading problems?

5. What are some of the linguistic causes of reading problems?

6. What are some of the nonlinguistic causes of reading problems?

7. Explain whether readers of other languages can display dyslexia.

8. What are some observations that may be early indicators of reading difficulties?

9. What are some basic things that teachers should know about teaching reading?

10. What are some basic things that beginning readers need to learn?

Activities

- *Strategies for Teaching Students With Reading Problems* **(pp. 103–104)**

Time: 30 minutes

Materials: Chart paper, markers, *How the Special Needs Brain Learns*, Second Edition

Organize the participants into job-alike groups as much as possible: Elementary teachers of the same grade level (or two) form a group. Group secondary teachers by subject area, others by job role (principals and assistant principals together, special education teachers together, etc.). No group should have more than five people. Each group selects a recorder. Give the groups chart paper and markers.

Ask the groups to open their books to pages 103–104. Give the groups 15 minutes to review those pages and to select and discuss the strategies which are most appropriate for their job roles. The recorders summarize their group's discussion on the chart paper and present their summary to the entire group.

Journal Writing: What are a few new strategies that I will use to help students with reading difficulties?

● *Reading Bingo*

Time: 20 minutes

Materials: Copies of the Reading Bingo game sheet for each participant.

This activity is an excellent review of the chapter. Have the participants read the instructions on the Reading Bingo game sheets as well as the information in the squares. Give them adequate time to review their notes and the chapter, including the "Strategies to Consider." Some participants like to become "experts" in a particular topic during the game.

After several minutes of review time, ask them to get up and find people who can complete the tasks in the boxes and initial them. Set a time limit of about 10 to 12 minutes, depending on the size of the group. Keep reminding them of how much time is left.

To increase motivation, you might have prizes for the first one, two, or three to get bingo. When the game is over, ask the participants to discuss in pairs or in groups how they could use a similar activity with their own students.

This would also be an appropriate time to clarify any confusion, misconceptions, or uncertainties that may have arisen when the participants were answering the questions in the bingo grid.

Reading Bingo

Directions: In this activity, the entire group gets up and moves around. Each person tries to find someone who can answer one of the questions in the box. The person who answers the question initials the box. The object is to get a bingo pattern (horizontally, vertically, or diagonally). No person may initial the same sheet twice. Time limit: 15 to 20 minutes, depending on the size of the group.

FIND A PERSON WHO IS ABLE TO

Compare phonological and phonemic awareness	Describe the visual processing system in reading	Explain the connection between vocabulary and reading	Discuss if dyslexia appears in other languages	Discuss how brain scans could diagnose dyslexia
Describe a social cause of reading problems	Explain a linguistic cause of reading problems	Describe a cultural cause of reading problems	Describe the auditory processing system in reading	Explain a nonlinguistic cause of reading problems
Explain the alphabetic principle	Name two indicators of dyslexia	Explain phonemic awareness	Describe reciprocal teaching	Describe story mapping
Describe the frontal lobe's role in reading	Describe developmental dyslexia	Explain why reading is not a natural ability	Explain deep orthography	Explain the response-to-instruction model
Explain how memory deficits affect reading	Explain what is meant by decoding in reading	Describe word-blindness	Explain the steps in the PASS Process	Explain shallow orthography

Chapter 6: Writing Disabilities

Summary

- Learning to write consists of integrating the consolidation of mental functions that select the content of the writing with the physical act of moving a writing instrument across a surface to form words. Writing involves the blending of attention, fine motor coordination, memory, visual processing, language, and higher-order thinking. Accomplishing this task requires visual memory for symbols, whole-word memory, and spelling rules.

- Writing requires a properly functioning central nervous system, intact receptive and expressive language skills, and the related cognitive operations. To write accurately and clearly also requires emotional stability; application of the concepts of organization and flow; an understanding of the rules of pronunciation, spelling, grammar, and syntax; visual and spatial organization; and simultaneous processing.

- Difficulties with writing can be environmental or they can stem from deficits within one or more of the neural networks needed for legible and clear writing to occur. Like reading, the brain does not perceive writing to be a survival skill, so the brain has no "writing centers" comparable to those for spoken language. Learning to write therefore requires direct instruction—it is not innate to the brain.

- In some schools, little time is given to formal instruction in handwriting. Some of the difficulties students experience with writing may be due to an unfortunate combination of learning the difficult skills of writing with very little practice. Now, students are questioning the need to write well because typing into a word-processing program seems so much easier.

- Spelling errors should not be seen as an impediment to writing but as an indication of the child's thought processes while making sense of letter-sound relationships. Research studies indicate that, with appropriate teacher intervention, invented spellings gradually come closer to conventional forms. Remember that practice eventually makes permanent. The consistent repetition of incorrect spellings will, in time, lead to their storage in long-term memory. Therefore, teachers should use strategies that will help children transform invented spelling into conventional spelling.

- Dysgraphia is a spectrum disorder describing major difficulties in mastering the sequence of movements necessary to write letters and numbers. The handwriting of students with dysgraphia is usually characterized by slow copying, inconsistencies in letter formation, mixtures of different letters and styles, and poor legibility. Teachers must realize that dysgraphia is a neurological disorder and is not the result of laziness, not caring, not trying, or just carelessness in writing.

- Dysgraphia is divided into three types: dyslexic, motor, and spatial. Dysgraphia can occur with other learning difficulties, such as dyslexia, ADHD, and auditory- and visual-processing disorders.

- Because students with writing disorders often lack confidence in their ability to write, educators working with these students need to help them regain confidence by using accommodation, modification, and remediation strategies.

Supplemental Information

It is important to emphasize that writing consists of two processes: (1) mentally composing content, and (2) physically transcribing words to paper. Different neural systems are involved in each process. Spend time carefully reviewing the diagram (by Alan Wing on page 120 of the book) that illustrates how these systems interact. Difficulties can arise in either or both processes.

Discussion Questions

1. What are some environmental causes of poor writing?

2. How should teachers deal with a student's invented spelling?

3. What are some neurological causes of poor writing?

4. Explain the three different types of dysgraphia, their symptoms, and possible causes.

5. What are some of the tests that can be used to diagnose dysgraphia?

6. With what other disorders has dysgraphia been associated?

7. Describe the seven traits of good writing included in the *6+1 Trait Writing Program*?

8. What are some ways that teachers can build confidence in students with writing disorders?

9. What are some accommodation strategies for students with writing disorders?

10. What are some modification strategies for students with writing disorders?

11. What are some remediation strategies for students with writing disorders?

12. Explain the three instructional components that consistently lead to improving student success in learning expressive writing?

Activity

● *Identifying Students With Writing Difficulties*

Time: 20–30 minutes

Materials: Chart paper, markers, *How the Special Needs Brain Learns,* Second Edition

Divide participants into discussion groups of four or five. Give each group chart paper and markers, and ask them to select a recorder. Project the following question on a screen or write it on chart paper:

Why is it that many students with writing difficulties do not get identified for special assistance?

Ask the groups to discuss this statement and to come up with some reasons that support or contradict the statement. The recorder lists the reasons on chart paper. When time is up, each recorder (or selected recorders, if there is a large number of groups) reports the results to the entire group. Summarize the major points made by the recorders.

Journal Writing: What will I do to raise my awareness of students with writing difficulties?

Chapter 7: Mathematical Disabilities

Summary

- Research appears to confirm that humans are born with a number sense. Functional MRI scans indicate that the parietal and frontal lobes are primarily involved in basic mental mathematics. Activation intensifies as the number size increases. Approximate calculations require larger cerebral areas than exact calculations, presumably because approximation requires more number manipulation. Other areas of the brain are recruited into action when dealing with more complex mathematics, such as in algebraic calculations and geometry.
- Imaging studies confirm that the brain areas responsible for calculations are different from those used in processing language. No matter how helpful language may be in developing mathematical ability, it is not necessary to calculation. Thus, students with mathematical difficulties may not necessarily have difficulties with language, and those with language problems may still be capable in mathematics.
- For decades, boys have consistently scored higher than girls on standardized mathematics tests, such as the Scholastic Aptitude Test (SAT) and the National Assessment of Educational Progress (NAEP). Male brains are about eight percent larger than female brains, and brain-imaging studies show that males seem to have an advantage in visual-spatial ability. But whether these differences translate into a genetic advantage for males

over females in mathematical processing remains to be proved. The belief that boys are much better at mathematics than girls is out of proportion to the data. Recent test results indicate that the gender gap is narrowing. These gender differences are not unchangeable, and a variety of teaching approaches and strategies may indeed compensate for them.

- About six to eight percent of school-age children have serious difficulty processing mathematics, about the same number as children who have serious reading problems. Persistent problems with processing numerical calculations is referred to as *dyscalculia*. Dyscalculia is a difficulty in conceptualizing numbers, number relationships, outcomes of numerical operations, and estimation, that is, what to expect as an outcome of an operation.

- Dyscalculia can be quantitative, which is a difficulty in counting and calculating; qualitative, which is a difficulty in the conceptualizing of mathematics processes and spatial sense; or mixed, which is the inability to integrate quantity and space.

- Types of dyscalculia include number-concept difficulties, counting-skill deficits, difficulties with arithmetic skills, procedural and memory disorders, and visual-spatial deficits.

- Dyscalculia has been associated with reading disorders, ADHD, and nonverbal learning disability (NLD).

- Diagnosing dyscalculia is not an easy task. Educators should examine the degree to which students with mathematics difficulties possess the prerequisite skills for learning mathematical operations. What skills are weak, and what can we do about that? They also should look at the mathematics curriculum to determine the types of instructional strategies that teachers are using.

- Diagnostic tools for assessing learning difficulties in mathematics include determining the student's level of cognitive awareness, the degree of language ability, and the mastery of prerequisite skills and concepts.

- Cognitive researchers suggest that students approach the study of mathematics with different learning styles that run the gamut from primarily quantitative to primarily qualitative. The implication of this research is that students are more likely to be successful in learning mathematics if teachers use instructional strategies that are compatible with the students' cognitive styles.

- Students with NLD have good verbal-processing skills but will have problems comprehending the visual and spatial components of mathematics skills and concepts, especially when dealing with geometric shapes and designs. They generally learn verbal information quickly, but may not be able to make sense of diagrams.

Supplemental Information

The notion that humans are probably born with a number sense has sparked a new wave of research into the nature of that innate ability. Scientists are examining the brain regions responsible for different mathematical operations, hoping to gain a greater understanding of how these operations work and what can go wrong. Of particular interest are the brain areas that do sequential counting and those that estimate the number of things in a group.

Recent studies have shown that some boys who have difficulties in algebra are really having trouble translating word problems into algebraic expressions. When given just the equations, most boys were able to solve the expressions correctly. Researchers suggest that teachers should spend much more time teaching mathematics as a second language, so students understand its unique terminology, syntax, and other linguistic elements.

Although dyscalculia can be associated in the same individual with other learning disorders, most dyscalculia is the result of specific disabilities in the numerical-processing areas of the brain, rather than of deficits in other cognitive abilities.

Discussion Questions

1. Discuss the instructional implications of this statement: Research appears to confirm that humans are born with a number sense.

2. What is the relationship between language learning and mathematical ability?

3. Discuss the long-standing observation that boys are apparently more successful at learning mathematics than girls.

4. What is dyscalculia and what are its symptoms?

5. What are some of the types of dyscalculia?

6. With what other disorders is dyscalculia associated?

7. Discuss the prerequisite skills associated with learning mathematics.

8. What are some of the diagnostic tools used for assessing learning difficulties in mathematics?

9. How do learning styles affect the learning of mathematics?

Activity

● *General Guidelines for Teaching Mathematics* (pp. 154–155)

Time: 20-30 minutes

Materials: Chart paper, markers, *How the Special Needs Brain Learns*, Second Edition

This activity is appropriate for all elementary and secondary teachers who teach mathematics, along with their supervisors and administrators. Organize the participants into discussion groups by grade level(s). Each group should select a recorder, and no group should have more than five to six people. Give the groups chart paper and markers.

Have the groups open their books to pages 154–155. Their task is to decide on a specific classroom-content example that would illustrate each of the 10 general guidelines for teaching mathematics. For example, for the first guideline, "Help students develop conceptual understanding and skills," the group should select a specific example from their grade-level mathematics curriculum and explain how they would link a concrete model to more abstract representations. Another option is to give a specific instructional strategy that would satisfy the intent of the guideline. For example, for the fifth guideline, "Build on children's strengths," suggest a specific instructional strategy that would accomplish this. When completed, ask if any participants would like to share one of their group's examples with the entire group.

Chapter 8: Emotional and Behavioral Disorders

Summary

- The human brain has learned that survival and emotional messages must have high priority when it filters through all the incoming signals from the body's senses. The brainstem monitors and regulates survival functions such as body temperature, respiratory rate, and blood pressure. Emotional messages are carried through and interpreted in the limbic area, usually with the help of the frontal lobe. These survival and emotional messages guide the individual's behavior, including directing its attention to a learning situation. Specifically, emotion drives attention and attention drives learning.

- Emotional attention comes before cognitive recognition. You can respond emotionally to a situation without the benefit of cognitive functions, such as thinking, reasoning, and consciousness.
- The thalamus receives all incoming sensory impulses (except smell) and directs them to other parts of the brain for further processing. Incoming sensory information to the thalamus can take two different routes to the amygdala. The quick route (called the *thalamic pathway*) sends the signals directly from the thalamus to the amygdala. The second possibility (called the *cortical pathway*) is for the thalamus to direct the signals first to the cerebral cortex (in the cerebrum) for cognitive processing and then to the amygdala. The time it takes for signals to travel along the two pathways is different. Which pathway the signals take could mean the difference between life and death. Disturbances in this dual pathway system can explain some abnormal behaviors.
- Different areas of the brain interpret specific emotions. The frontal cortex of the left hemisphere deals with positive emotions; the right frontal cortex is concerned with negative emotions. People who normally have right hemisphere preference tend to have basically anxious and fearful approaches to life. Those with left hemisphere preference exhibit a more confident approach.
- Anxiety serves a useful purpose in that it signals us that something needs to be corrected in our environment. Emotional stability is the result of the interactions between the emotion-generating amygdala and the emotion-inhibiting left frontal cortex. Both the amygdala and left frontal cortex need to be functioning properly for this balance to be maintained and, thus, for good mental health. If either one is malfunctioning, then the person's behavior likely will be abnormal.
- The human brain is programmed to deal first with its owner's survival and emotional needs. Therefore, the brain is unlikely to attend to any other task until it is assured that these needs have been met and that the environment poses no threat. In schools, this means that students are not going to care about the curriculum unless they feel physically safe and emotionally secure.
- Common anxiety disorders include phobias, generalized anxiety disorder (GAD), panic disorder, obsessive-compulsive disorder, (OCD), and posttraumatic stress disorder (PTSD). Anxiety disorders are thought to be caused mainly by malfunctions in the brain's amygdala.
- Depressive disorders include major depressive disorder, dysthymia, and bipolar disorder. The causes of these disorders are genetics, events occurring in the individual's environment, and events occurring inside the body.

- Other emotional and behavioral disorders include ADHD, oppositional-defiant disorder, conduct disorder, eating disorders, and autism.
- Brain-imaging studies and other experiments have confirmed that child abuse can cause permanent damage to the neural structure and function of the brain. Researchers now suspect that the stress associated with childhood abuse trigger hormonal changes that rewire the child's brain to deal with a malevolent world. This may explain why victims of child abuse can become abusers themselves as they age. Victims of childhood abuse may suffer from anxiety, depression, suicidal thoughts, or posttraumatic stress. Outwardly, they may display aggression, delinquency, hyperactivity, or impulsivity.
- Researchers suggest that educators consider three areas for improving the identification and treatment of students with emotional and behavioral disorders. The first area is developmental psychopathology, which holds that the course of these disorders is determined by a variety of early genetic, biologic, and environmental factors. The second area involves psychiatric comorbidity, the recognition that emotional and behavioral disorders may be preceded by other psychiatric problems. A third area for consideration is psychopharmacology. Special education teachers and general educators should be aware of how medication for psychiatric disorders has become an effective intervention, especially when combined with behavioral interventions.

Supplemental Information

According to the U.S. Surgeon General's Office, the number of children diagnosed with emotional and behavioral problems has nearly doubled in the past 10 years to more than 20 percent of the student population. This alarming increase is likely due to both better diagnostic tools as well as actual increases in incidence from genetic and environmental causes.

This chapter notes that one of the more significant contributors to emotional and behavioral problems is stress. And one of the prime causes of stress in students is lack of sleep. Adequate sleep is critical for mental and physical health. The encoding of information into the long-term memory sites occurs during sleep. When we sleep, the brain reviews the events and tasks of the day, storing them more securely than at the time we originally processed them. Thus, adequate sleep is vital to the memory-storage process, especially for young learners. Most teenagers need 8 to 9 hours of sleep each night, but only about 20 percent are actually getting that amount. Several factors are responsible for eroding sleep time. In the morning, high schools start earlier, teens spend more time grooming, and some travel long distances to school. At the end of the day, there are athletic and social events, part-time jobs, home-work, television, and video games. Add to this the shift in teens' body clocks that tends to keep them up later, and the average sleep time is more like 5 to 6 hours.

The problem is becoming so prevalent in middle and high schools that some neuroscientists and psychiatrists are convinced that it is a chronic disorder of the adolescent population. Called Delayed Sleep Phase Disorder (DSPD), it is characterized by a persistent pattern that includes difficulty falling asleep at night and getting up in the morning, fatigue during the day, and alertness at night. Caused mainly by the shift in the adolescent's sleep-wake cycle, DSPD is aggravated by other conditions, such as anxiety and too much caffeine.

Most of the encoding of information and skills into long-term storage is believed to occur during the rapid-eye movement (REM) phases. During the normal sleep time of 8 to 9 hours, five REM cycles occur. Adolescents getting just 5 to 6 hours of sleep lose out on the last two REM cycles, thereby reducing the amount of time the brain has to consolidate information and skills into long-term storage. This sleep deprivation not only disturbs the memory storage process but it puts the body under stress and can lead to other problems as well. Students may nod off in class or become irritable. Worse, their decreased alertness due to fatigue can lead to accidents in school and in their cars.

Students who get less sleep are more likely to get poorer grades in school than students who sleep longer. Sleep-deprived students also had more daytime sleepiness, depressed moods, and behavioral problems. It is important to remind students of the significance of sleep to their mental and physical health and to encourage them to reexamine their daily activities to provide for adequate sleep.

Discussion Questions

1. Explain the thalamic and cortical pathways for emotional signals.

2. What conditions provide physical safety for students and staff?

3. What conditions provide emotional security for students and staff?

4. Describe the most common types of anxiety disorders.

5. What are the causes of anxiety disorders and how can they be treated?

6. Describe the most common types of depressive disorders.

7. What are the causes of depressive disorders and how can they be treated?

8. Explain what kinds of emotional and behavioral problems can result from childhood abuse.

9. Describe the three areas that researchers suggest educators consider for improving the identification and treatment of students with emotional and behavioral disorders.

Activity

● *Establishing a Positive Emotional Climate in the Classroom* (pp. 172–173)

Time: 25 minutes, including reading time

Materials: Paper, pens, *How the Special Needs Brain Learns*, Second Edition

　　Ask the participants to read *Establishing a Positive Emotional Climate in the Classroom* on pages 172–173. When they have completed the reading, they should write down at least two things that they purposefully do now to create a positive emotional climate in their classrooms, and at least one new one they will try in the future. Administrators can write down how they create (or will create) a positive climate in their schools or in the central office. Allow about 5 minutes for this. Then ask the participants to walk across the room and, working in pairs, review their responses with a partner, explaining why they chose these particular strategies. Provide an opportunity for participants to share their thoughts with the entire group.

　　Alternative activity: Ask the participants to write down two student behavioral problems they have recently encountered in their classrooms or schools, and briefly describe how they dealt with them. They should also reflect on whether, as a result of reading this chapter, they would take the same or different course of action if confronted with those same behavior problems today. Why? Then ask the participants to walk across the room and, working in pairs, review the behavioral encounters with a partner, explaining why they would choose to respond in the same or in a different way, and why. Provide an opportunity for participants to share their thoughts with the entire group.

Journal Writing: What are at least two strategies that I will purposefully use to maintain a positive emotional climate in my classroom/school/central office?

Alternative activity: As a result of reading this chapter, why am I likely to respond in the same/different way as before when confronted with a particular behavior problem?

Chapter 9: Autism Spectrum Disorders

Summary

- Autism spectrum disorders (ASD) affect about 1 in 166 children, and four out of five are males. Are more children developing ASD or are we just getting better at finding those who already have it? Many experts say it is both.
- Pervasive developmental disorders (PDD) appear when several neural networks malfunction early in a child's life. PDDs include autistic disorder (classic autism), Asperger syndrome, pervasive developmental disorder—not otherwise specified (PDD-NOS), and two rare forms known as Rett syndrome, and childhood disintegrative disorder. All these disorders are characterized by varying degrees of impairment in communication skills, social interactions, and restricted, repetitive and stereotyped patterns of behavior. Each disorder is lifelong and can run the gamut from mild to severe.
- The prevalence of ASD demonstrates the importance of early and more accurate screening for symptoms. The earlier the disorder is diagnosed, the sooner the child can be helped through treatment interventions.
- Symptoms of ASD will appear in individual children differently. The symptoms usually appear before 3 years of age, but parents may notice the hints of future problems from birth. Between 12- and 36-months-old, the differences in the way they react to people and other unusual behaviors become apparent.
- In ASD, the brain seems unable to balance the senses appropriately. Thus, many children with ASD are highly attuned or even painfully sensitive to certain sounds, textures, tastes, and smells. Loud and intrusive sounds will cause these children to cover their ears and scream.
- Many children with autistic disorder and PDD-NOS have some degree of mental impairment. Individuals with Asperger syndrome however, have average to above average intelligence.
- Fragile X syndrome is the most common inherited form of mental retardation, and it affects about two to five percent of people with ASD. If a child with ASD also has Fragile X, there is a one-in-two chance that boys born to the same parents will have the syndrome.
- Most children with ASD have greater difficulty recalling verbal information compared to typically developing children. However, in studies involving working memory, individuals with high-functioning ASD (Asperger syndrome) solved problems involving spatial working memory at least as well as, or better than,

the control group. Apparently, working-memory deficits in ASD affect verbal-memory systems more than visual-spatial memory.

- The diagnosis for ASD involves two stages. The first stage is a screening process using parental questionnaires and clinical observations about a child's social and communicative development within medical settings. If the screening process shows possible indicators of ASD, further evaluation is needed. The second stage is a comprehensive evaluation by a team of professionals who diagnose children with ASD. Specialists evaluate language and social behavior, talk with parents about the child's developmental milestones, and test for certain genetic and neurological problems. A hearing test should also be performed.

- The exact causes of ASD are unknown. Most experts now agree that ASD is associated with abnormal brain developments that occur in part as a result of genetic factors. Major areas of research include studies of the size of brain structures, genetic mutations, levels of neurotransmitters, effects of mirror neurons, the extreme male theory, and mercury toxicity.

- About 10 percent of people with ASD display remarkable abilities known as *savant skills*. Not all people with savant skills have ASD. Researchers suspect these skills are a result of the brain's ability to process incoming information in its context, that is, to put parts together into a meaningful whole. Because this ability is weak in people with ASD, it may explain why they focus on details and parts at the expense of global meaning. Savant skills may also be a result of the uneven development of the brain's hemispheres.

- Asperger syndrome is a developmental disorder with many of the same symptoms of autistic disorder. It is often referred to as a mild form of ASD because people with Asperger syndrome generally have better communication skills and have higher mental functioning than those with typical ASD. Asperger syndrome is a lifelong condition. Some experts suggest that the next edition of the *DSM* should remove Asperger syndrome as a separate disorder and designate children with those symptoms as having high-functioning autism.

- At present, there is no cure for ASD, nor do children outgrow it. Early intervention, special education support, and medication are helping children and adolescents with ASD lead more normal lives. Medications alleviate some of the symptoms and therapy can help a child to learn, communicate, and interact with others in productive ways. Parental involvement is a major factor in treatment success. Parents work with teachers and therapists to identify the behaviors to be changed and the skills to be taught. Another effective treatment is applied behavior analysis, which reduces inappropriate behavior and increases communication, learning, and appropriate social behavior in individuals with ASD. This technique is tedious and time-consuming, but if started at an early age, some experts believe the process could actually rewire the young brain.

- Although ASD has long been defined by its behavioral symptoms, researchers are now focusing on what goes wrong in the brain to cause those behaviors. Genetic variations associated with ASD may provide a more accurate diagnostic tool for the future. It may even lead to early interventions during infancy.

Supplemental Information

The incidence of autism in the United States appears to be increasing. But is it an epidemic? Even as scientists try to figure out why autism cases are rising, there is a continuing debate over whether the rise is real. One problem is that studies of autism prevalence rarely target broad populations. They tend to focus on defined geographic areas, such as a state. Thus, they may not accurately reflect the prevalence nationwide. California, for example, reported a 273 percent increase in autism during the 10-year period from 1994 to 2004. Researchers do not believe this reflects the national rate of incidence. Better data will be needed before this debate can be resolved.

Discussion Questions

1. What disorders are included under the category of Autism Spectrum Disorders (ASD)?

2. Describe the major symptoms that people with ASD display.

3. Why do you think the number of children diagnosed with ASD has increased so rapidly in the past 10 years?

4. What are some possible causes of ASD?

5. Explain what is meant by "savant skills."

6. What are the similarities and differences between Asperger syndrome and autism?

7. Explain some of the current treatments for ASD.

Activities

- *Interventions for Children and Adolescents With Autism Spectrum Disorder* **(pp. 194–195)**

Time: 30 minutes

Materials: Paper, pens, *How the Special Needs Brain Learns*, Second Edition

This is a cooperative learning strategy known as jigsaw. Divide the participants into groups of four. These are the jigsaw groups. Ask the group members to number off one through four and to open their books to pages 194–195. There are four interventions described in those pages. Ask the group members to read only the intervention assigned to them. The assignments are

> Member 1: Applied Behavioral Analysis (ABA)
> Member 2: Discrete Trial Teaching (DTT)
> Member 3: Pivotal Response Training (PRT)
> Member 4: Learning Experiences: An Alternative Program for
> Preschoolers and Parents (LEAP)

Remind participants to concentrate only on the segment assigned to them. Give them time to read their segment at least twice and become familiar with it. There is no need for them to memorize it. Form temporary "expert groups" by having one member from each jigsaw group join other members assigned to the same segment. Limit each expert group to five or six people. Give the members in these expert groups time to discuss the main points of their segment and to rehearse the presentations they will make to their jigsaw group. Bring the members back into their jigsaw groups of four. Ask members to present their segment to the original jigsaw group, starting with Member 1, and in numerical order through Member 4. Encourage others in the group to ask questions for clarification.

Journal Writing: Briefly describe the four interventions for individuals with autism spectrum disorders.

● *True-False Questions About Autism Spectrum Disorder*

Time: 15-20 minutes

Materials: Copy of the following list of true-false questions about autism spectrum disorders (ASD).

1. T F Anyone with ASD is a genius or has an unusual or amazing talent.

2. T F Chelation is an ASD treatment accepted by the scientific community.

3. T F Children with ASD cannot learn basic cognitive skills.

4. T F Most children with ASD never learn to talk.

5. T F ASD is a childhood disorder.

6. T   F   People with ASD are unable to develop personal relationships or feel emotions.

7. T   F   Causes of autism include allergies and chemical imbalances that can be cured by special diets and nutritional supplements.

8. T   F   Children with ASD never make eye contact.

9. T   F   All individuals with ASD do not like to be touched.

Provide a copy of the true-false questions to each participant. Ask them to work alone and decide whether each statement is essentially true or false. When they have completed the instrument, have them walk across the room and, working in pairs, share their answers with a partner. After suitable time for discussion, ask if any pairs would like to share their comments with the entire group. At some point reveal to the group that all the statements are false.

Chapter 10: Putting It All Together

Summary

- Four important areas that ought to be considered when working with students who have learning difficulties include identification, accommodation, motivation, and communication.
- Often, the regular classroom teacher is the first to spot learning problems. An assessment inventory is useful in determining whether learning problems are temporary or persistent. The results of the inventory, teacher observations, and student performance may indicate that a more formal assessment of the student's achievement is needed to determine if a learning disability exists. Many schools use an ability (IQ)-achievement discrepancy model to identify the presence of a learning disability. Responsiveness to Intervention (RTI) is another method for identifying learning disabilities. In RTI, students who do not respond to intensive intervention would be identified as having a learning disability. Some researchers recommend that the RTI model be expanded to a framework that includes findings from neuroscience on how the brain develops and learns.
- To accommodate students with learning disabilities, educators should learn about learning; design a learning profile for each student with learning problems; modify the learning environment, their instructional strategies, and curriculum materials; use group instruction; adjust time demands; deal with inappropriate behavior; and modify homework assignments.

- To motivate students with learning difficulties, educators should structure activities for success, set realistic expectations, link success to effort, communicate positive expectations, and demonstrate noncontingent acceptance.
- Ways to communicate with parents include developing and sharing a daily and weekly journal, scheduling periodic parent-teacher meetings, providing a duplicate set of textbooks for home use during the school year, providing weekly progress reports to parents, mailing (or e-mailing) the parents a schedule of class and homework assignments, and explaining clearly the school's grading policy and any adaptations that were made for the student.

Discussion Questions

1. Explain some methods used to identify whether students have a learning disability.

2. What are some ways to accommodate students with learning difficulties?

3. How can educators motivate students with learning difficulties?

4. Why is communicating with parents of students with learning problems so important? What are some ways of communicating?

Workshop Evaluation Form

Content

- How well did this workshop meet its goals?

- How will you apply what you learned during this workshop in your daily professional life?

- What professional support will you need to implement what you have learned from this workshop?

- How well did the topics explored in this workshop meet a specific need in your school or district?

- How relevant was this topic to your professional life?

Process

- How well did the instructional techniques and activities facilitate your understanding of the topic?

- How can you incorporate the activities learned today into your daily professional life?

- Were a variety of learning experiences included in the workshop?

- Was any particular activity memorable? What made it stand out?

Context

- Were the facilities conducive to learning?

- Were the accommodations adequate for the activities involved?

Overall

- Overall, how successful would you consider this workshop? Please include a brief comment or explanation.

Additional Comments

SOURCE: Adapted from *Evaluating Professional Development* by Thomas R. Guskey, Corwin Press, Inc., 2000

CORWIN PRESS

The Corwin Press logo—a raven striding across an open book—represents the union of courage and learning. Corwin Press is committed to improving education for all learners by publishing books and other professional development resources for those serving the field of PreK–12 education. By providing practical, hands-on materials, Corwin Press continues to carry out the promise of its motto: **"Helping Educators Do Their Work Better."**